PIANO · VOCAL · CHORDS

THE
TV SONGS
BIG BOOK

APR 1 8 2013

10-18 (8)

D1595153

Alfred Publishing Co., Inc.
16320 Roscoe Blvd., Suite 100
P.O. Box 10003
Van Nuys, CA 91410-0003
alfred.com

ISBN-10: 0-7390-4580-6
ISBN-13: 978-0-7390-4580-0

CONTENTS

CONTENTS

Theme from "GROWING PAINS"

AS LONG AS WE GOT EACH OTHER

Words by
JOHN BETTIS

Music by
STEVE DORFF

As Long As We Got Each Other - 4 - 1

6

ing   we can take an - y - thing that comes our   way,___ ba - by,

rain or shine,_____   all ___ the time,_____   we got each oth - er

shar - ing the laugh - ter   and love.

love.

D.S. % al Coda ⊕

7

Based on a Theme from the Warner Bros. TV Movie "THE THORN BIRDS"

ANYWHERE THE HEART GOES

(Meggie's Theme)

Words by
WILL JENNINGS

Music by
HENRY MANCINI

Anywhere the Heart Goes - 3 - 1

1

From the TV Show "COPS"

BAD BOYS

Words and Music by
IAN LEWIS

Bad__ boys, what-'cha want, what-'cha want,

what-'cha gon-na do__ when__ Sher-iff John Brown__ come for you?

Bad Boys - 5 - 1

12

14

know some - times_____ you wan-na let go._____ Bad

Chorus:

Repeat ad lib. and fade

boys, bad boys, what-'cha gon-na do, what-'cha gon-na do when they come for you? Bad

Verse 2:
You chuck it on that one,
you chuck it on this one,
you chuck it on your mother
and you chuck it on your father.
You chuck it on your brother
and you chuck it on your sister,
you chuck it on that one
and you chuck it on me.
(To Chorus:)

Verse 3:
Nobody naw give you no breaks,
police naw give you no breaks,
soldier naw give you no breaks,
not even your idren naw give you no breaks.
(To Chorus:)

Theme From "GILLIGAN'S ISLAND" TV Series

THE BALLAD OF GILLIGAN'S ISLE

Words and Music by
SHERWOOD SCHWARTZ and GEORGE WYLE

The Ballad of Gilligan's Isle - 2 - 1

THE BALLAD OF DAVY CROCKETT

Words by
TOM BLACKBURN

Music by
GEORGE BRUNS

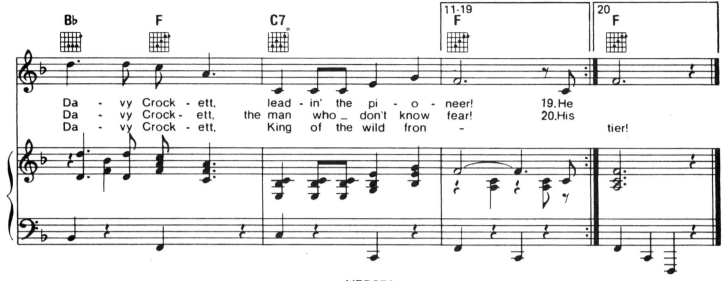

Da - vy Crock - ett, lead - in' the pi - o - neer!   19.He
Da - vy Crock - ett, the man who _ don't know fear!   20.His
Da - vy Crock - ett, King of the wild fron -   tier!

VERSES

4.
Andy Jackson is our gen'ral's name,
His reg'lar soldiers we'll put to shame,
Them redskin varmints us Volunteers'll tame,
'Cause we got the guns with the sure-fire aim.
Davy — Davy Crockett,
The champion of us all!

5.
Headed back to war from the ol' home place,
But Red Stick was leadin' a merry chase,
Fightin' an' burnin' at a devil's pace
South to the swamps on the Florida Trace.
Davy — Davy Crockett,
Trackin' the redskins down!

6.
Fought single-handed through the Injun War
Till the Creeks was whipped an' peace was in store,
An' while he was handlin' this risky chore,
Made hisself a legend for evermore.
Davy — Davy Crockett,
King of the wild frontier!

7.
He give his word an' he give his hand
That his Injun friends could keep their land,
An' the rest of his life he took the stand
That justice was due every redskin band.
Davy — Davy Crockett,
Holdin' his promise dear!

8.
Home fer the winter with his family,
Happy as squirrels in the ol' gum tree,
Bein' the father he wanted to be,
Close to his boys as the pod an' the pea.
Davy — Davy Crockett,
Holdin' his young 'uns dear!

9.
But the ice went out an' the warm winds came
An' the meltin' snow showed tracks of game,
An' the flowers of Spring filled the woods with flame,
An' all of a sudden life got too tame.
Davy — Davy Crockett,
Headin' on West again!

10.
Off through the woods we're riding' along,
Makin' up yarns an' singin' a song,
He's ringy as a b'ar an' twict as strong,
An' knows he's right 'cause he ain't often wrong.
Davy — Davy Crockett,
The man who don't know fear!

11.
Lookin' fer a place where the air smells clean,
Where the trees is tall an' the grass is green,
Where the fish is fat in an untouched stream,
An' the teemin' woods is a hunter's dream.
Davy — Davy Crockett,
Lookin' fer Paradise!

12.
Now he'd lost his love an' his grief was gall,
In his heart he wanted to leave it all,
An' lose himself in the forests tall,
But he answered instead his country's call.
Davy — Davy Crockett,
Beginnin' his campaign!

13.
Needin' his help they didn't vote blind,
They put in Davy 'cause he was their kind,
Sent up to Nashville the best they could find,
A fightin' spirit an' a thinkin' mind.
Davy — Davy Crockett,
Choice of the whole frontier!

14.
The votes were counted an' he won hands down,
So they sent him off to Washin'ton town
With his best dress suit still his buckskins brown,
A livin' legend of growin' renown.
Davy — Davy Crockett,
The Canebrake Congressman!

15.
He went off to Congress an' served a spell,
Fixin' up the Gover'ment an' laws as well,
Took over Washin'ton so we heered tell
An' patched up the crack in the Liberty Bell.
Davy — Davy Crockett,
Seein' his duty clear!

16.
Him an' his jokes travelled all through the land,
An' his speeches made him friends to beat the band,
His politickin' was their favorite brand
An' everyone wanted to shake his hand.
Davy — Davy Crockett,
Helpin' his legend grow!

17.
He knew when he spoke he sounded the knell
Of his hopes for White House an' fame as well,
But he spoke out strong so hist'ry books tell
An patched up the crack in the Liberty Bell.
Davy — Davy Crockett,
Seein' his duty clear!

The Ballad of Davy Crockett - 3 - 3

A Greenway Production in Association with 20th Century-Fox TV for ABC-TV

BATMAN THEME

Words and Music by
NEAL HEFTI

Batman Theme - 3 - 1

23

BEST FRIEND

Words and Music by
HARRY NILSSON

26

Best Friend - 3 - 3

CAGNEY & LACEY THEME

Music by
BILL CONTI

Cagney & Lacey Theme - 3 - 1

28

From Warner Bros. Television's The O.C.

CALIFORNIA

Words and Music by
AL JOLSON, B.G. DESYLVA, JOSEPH MEYER,
JASON SCHWARTZMAN and ALEX GREENWALD

32

nia! Cal - i-for - nia! Here_ we come!_____

Oh!_____

mf

dim.

34

CHARLIE'S ANGELS
(Main Title)

By
JACK ELLIOT and
ALLYN FERGUSON

Charlie's Angels - 3 - 1

36

Charlie's Angels - 3 - 2

Theme from the Lorimar Productions, Inc. Televison Series "Dallas"

DALLAS

Music by
JERROLD IMMEL

Dallas - 4 - 1

Coda

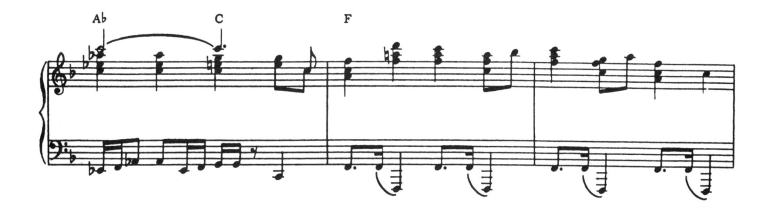

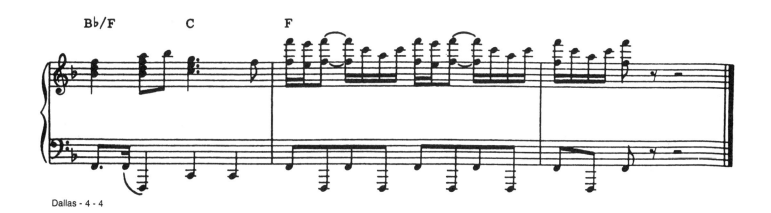

Dallas - 4 - 4

Theme from the TV Series "DANIEL BOONE"

DANIEL BOONE

Lyrics by
VERA MATSON

Music by
LIONEL NEWMAN

Moderately *(with vigor)*

1. Dan - iel Boone was a man! Yes, a big
2. Dan - iel Boone was a man! Yes, a big

man! With an eye like an ea-gle and as tall as a moun-tain was
man! With a whoop and a hol-ler he c'd mow down a for-est of

he!_____
trees!_____

Dan - iel Boone was a
Dan - iel Boone was a

Daniel Boone - 4 - 1

44

Extra lyrics for bridge

Well he always kept his rifle in reach
And a better shot never was!
He c'd shoot a fat fly clean off'n a peach
And never touch the fuzz
Daniel Boone was a man!
Yes, a BIG man!
And he fought for America
To make all Americans free!
What a Boone! What a do-er!
What a dream-come-er-true-er was he!

With a knife and a gun he never did fail
There was nothin' he could not tame!
He blazed a big wide Liberty trail
Through hist'ry's Hall of Fame
Daniel Boone was a man!
Yes, a BIG man!
And he fought for America
To make all Americans free!
What a Boone! What a do-er!
What a dream-come-er-true-er was he!

DREAMLOVE

Words and Music by
ROXANNE SEEMAN and BILLIE HUGHES

48

50

Theme from the Warner Bros. Animated TV Series "FREE WILLY"

FREE WILLY

Words and Music by
MICHAEL KAMEN

Free Willy - 3 - 1

just as long as you are free _____ Wil - ly, _____

my heart has a home.

Just as long as you are free _____ Wil - ly, _____

my heart has a home.

rit.

ER
(Main Theme)

Composed by
JAMES NEWTON HOWARD

ER - 2 - 1

55

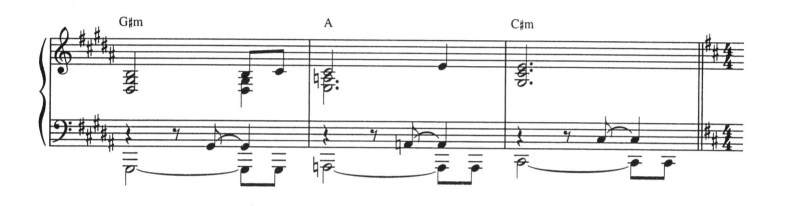

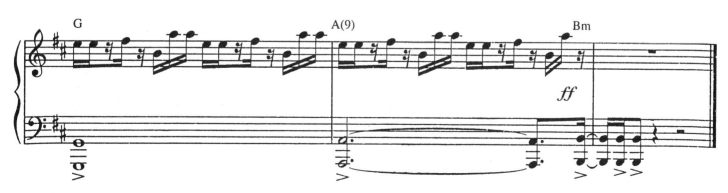

ER - 2 - 2

From the CBS Television Series "AS THE WORLD TURNS"

EVERY BEAT OF MY HEART

Words and Music by
BRIAN McKNIGHT and EARL ROSE

Every Beat of My Heart - 6 - 1

58

EVERYBODY LOVES RAYMOND
(Main Title)

By
RICK MAROTTA
and TERRY TROTTER

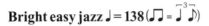

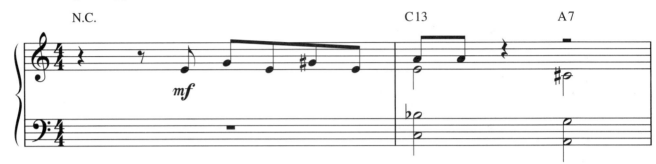

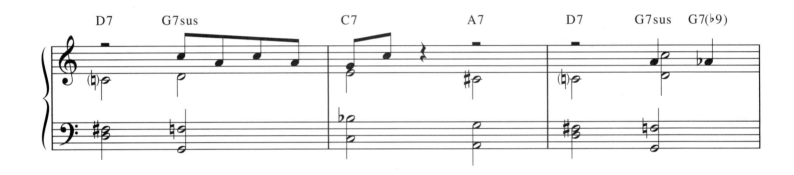

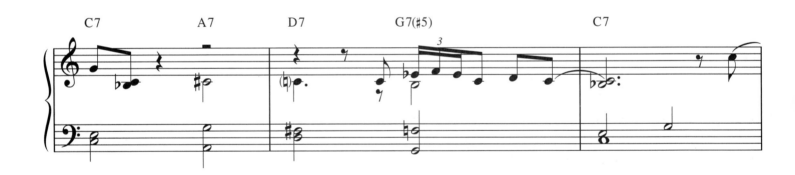

Everybody Loves Raymond - 2 - 1

Theme From TriStar Television's "MAD ABOUT YOU"

FINAL FRONTIER

Words and Music by
PAUL REISER and DON WAS

(MEET) THE FLINTSTONES
from THE FLINTSTONES

Words and Music by
WILLIAM HANNA, JOSEPH BARBERA
and HOYT CURTIN

68

THE FUGITIVE

By
PETE RUGULO

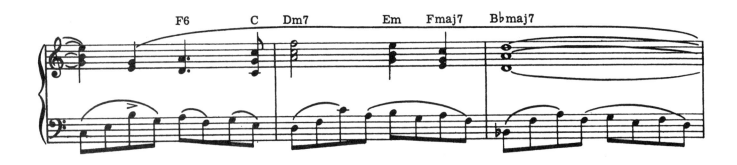

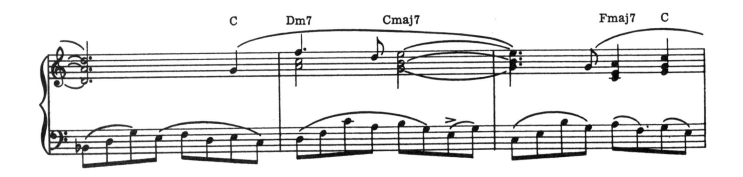

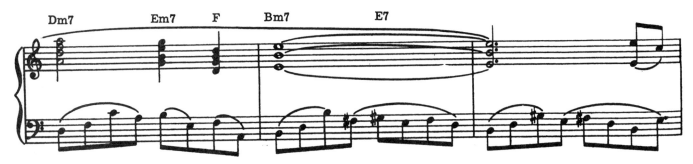

The Fugitive - 2 - 2

GO GO POWER RANGERS

Words and Music by
HAIM SABAN and SHUKI LEVY

Go Go Power Rangers - 9 - 1

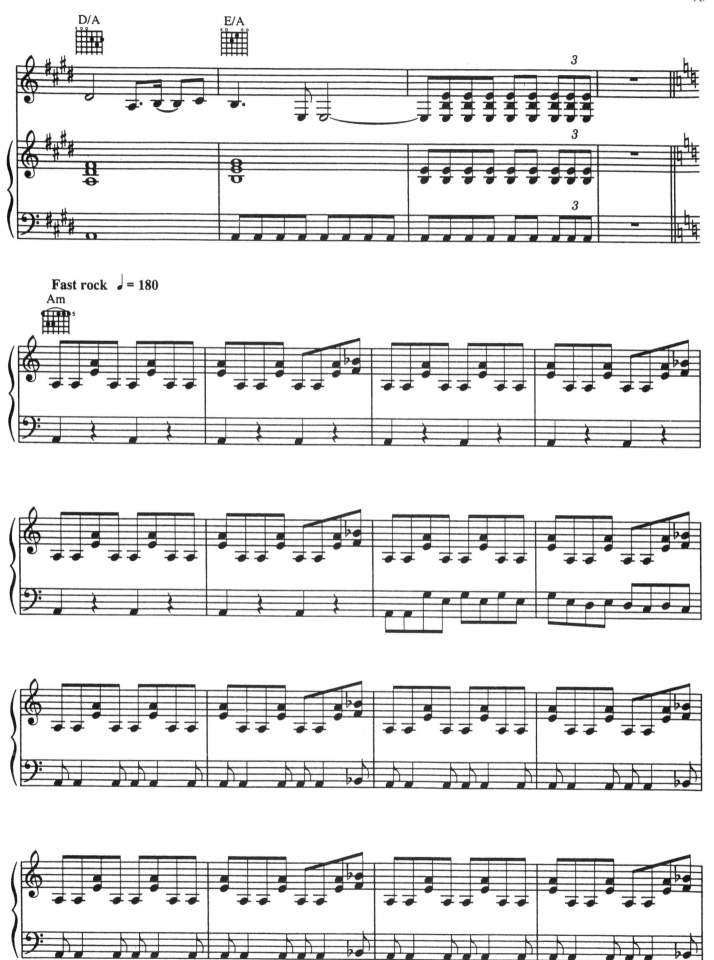

74

1. They've got a
2. They know the

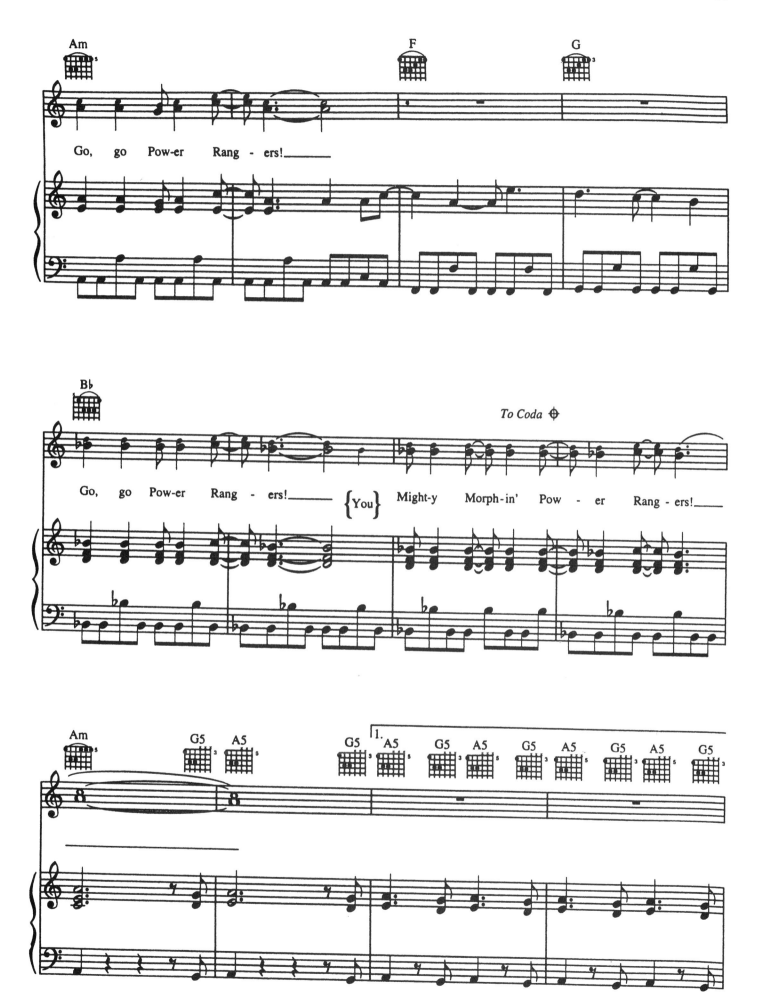

78

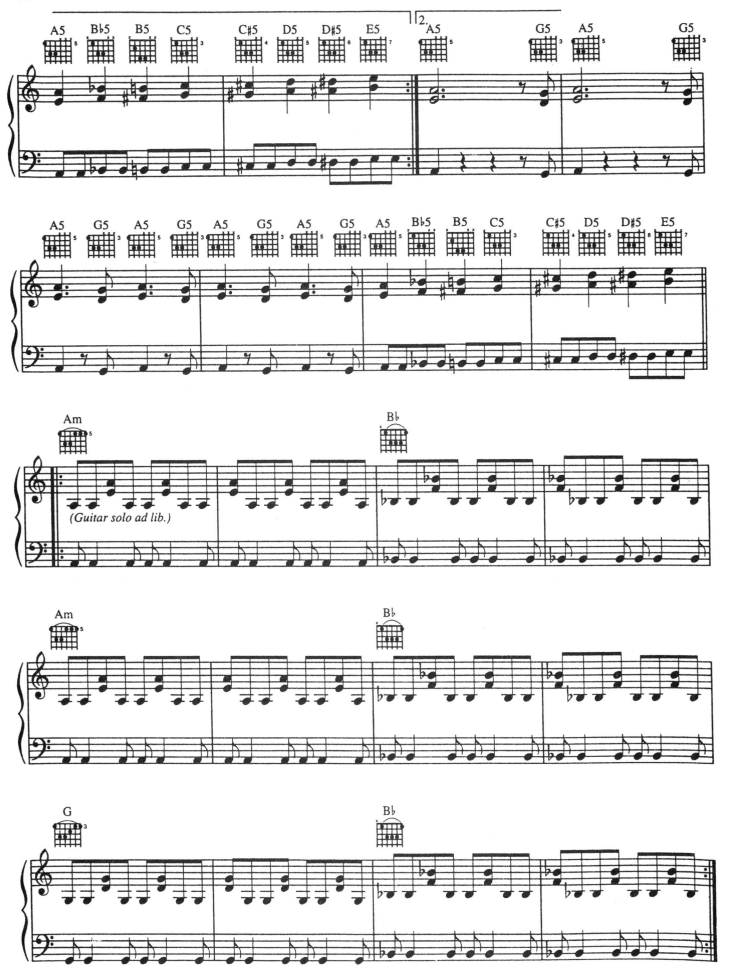

D.S. % al Coda

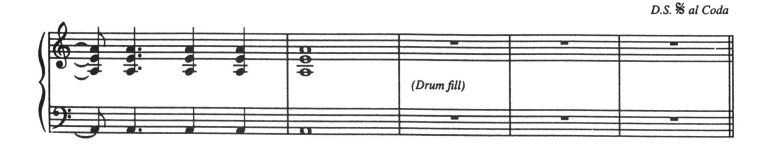

(Drum fill)

er Rang - ers! Go, Go Pow-er Rang - ers!_____

Go, go Pow-er Rang - ers!_____

HIGH UPON THIS LOVE
(Love Theme From "The Bold and the Beautiful")

Lyrics by DIONNE WARWICK,
ANDREW WEITZ and DAVID ELLIOT

Music by DAVID KURTZ,
JACK ALLOCCO and BRADLEY P. BELL

High Upon This Love - 5 - 1

84

High Upon This Love - 5 - 4

Verse 2:
They say love is truly blind,
And it will stand the test of time.
A love truly meant to be,
Two hearts as one so free.
I give my all.
You hold the key.
(To Chorus:)

Verse 3:
You are my shining light
In the shadow of the night.
It's the love that you see
In every part of me.
One touch, you set me free.

Verse 4:
Let's hold on to what we have,
'Cause love so often dies.
Won't be fooled by fantasy,
'Cause I believe in you and me,
And we'll never say goodbye.
(To Chorus:)

Theme from the TV Series "THE DUKES OF HAZZARD"

GOOD OL' BOYS

Moderately Fast, with half-time feel

Words and Music by
WAYLON JENNINGS

Verse 2:
Straight'nin' the curve, flat'nin' the hills.
Someday the mountains might get 'em,
But the law never will. *(To Chorus:)*

Verses 3 & 4: *(Instrumental solos)*

Verse 5:
I'm a good ol' boy.
You know, my momma loves me,
But she don't understand.
They keep a'showin' my hands,
And not my face on T.V.
(Laughs) Hah, hah.

Theme from the Greenway/20th Century-Fox TV Production "GREEN HORNET"

GREEN HORNET THEME

Words and Music by
BILLY MAY

Green Hornet Theme - 2 - 1

HUCKLEBERRY HOUND
from the Cartoon Television Series

Words and Music by WILLIAM HANNA,
JOSEPH BARBERA and HOYT CURTIN

Huckleberry Hound - 2 - 1

I WANT TO BE THE ONE

(from "Who Wants to Marry My Dad")

Words and Music by
EARL ROSE and PAMELA HUGHES

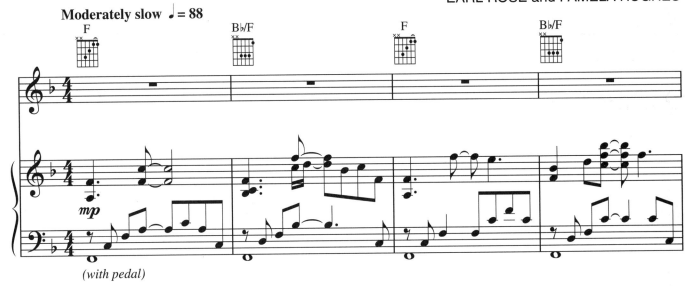

(with pedal)

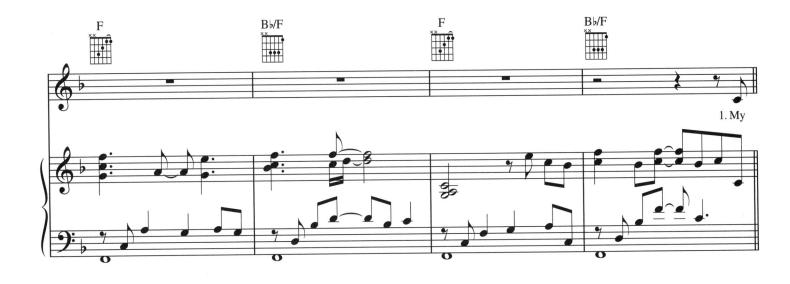

1. My

Verse 1:

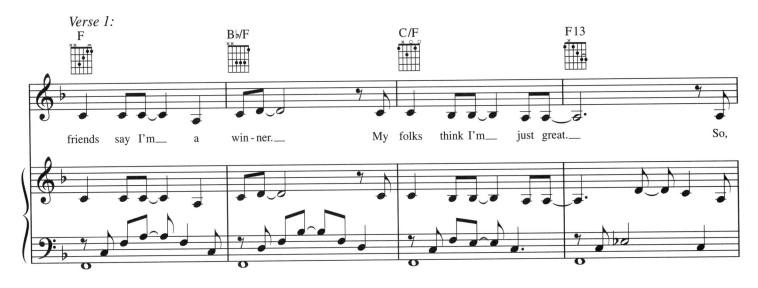

friends say I'm__ a win-ner.__ My folks think I'm__ just great.__ So,

I Want to Be the One - 4 - 1

94

I Want to Be the One - 4 - 3

Verse 3:
Everyone tells me "keep tryin'."
Just toss my hat in the ring.
But every time I do
It's just the same old thing.
(To Chorus:)

I'LL BE THERE FOR YOU

(Theme from "Friends")

Words by
DAVID CRANE, MARTA KAUFFMAN,
ALLEE WILLIS, PHIL SOLEM
and DANNY WILDE

Music by
MICHAEL SKLOFF

Fast rock ♩= 190

1. So, no one told you life was gon-na be this way.
2. You're still in bed at ten and work be-gan at eight.

Your job's a joke, you're broke, your
You've burned your break - fast, so far, your

I'll Be There for You - 6 - 1

98

rain starts to pour. I'll be there for you

like I've been there be-fore. I'll be

there for you 'cause you're there for me,

To Coda 1. 2.

too.

Bridge:

No one could ev-

* Guitar fill reads 8va.

I'll Be There for You - 6 - 3

er know— me, no one could ev - er see— me.

Seems you're the on - ly one— who knows— what it's

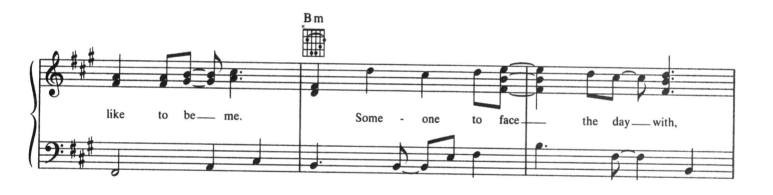

like to be— me. Some - one to face— the day— with,

make it through all— the rest— with, some - one I'll al -

From the Television Show "AS THE WORLD TURNS"

IF THIS ISN'T LOVE

Words and Music by
GLORIA SKLEROV and STEVE DORFF

If This Isn't Love - 4 - 1

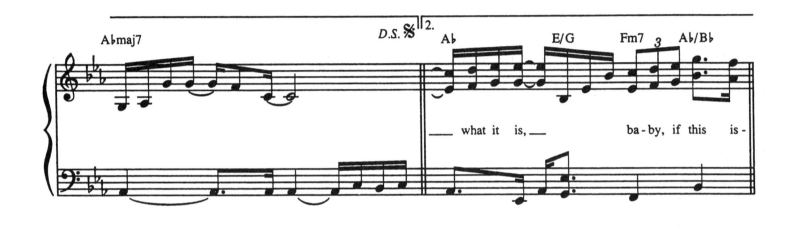

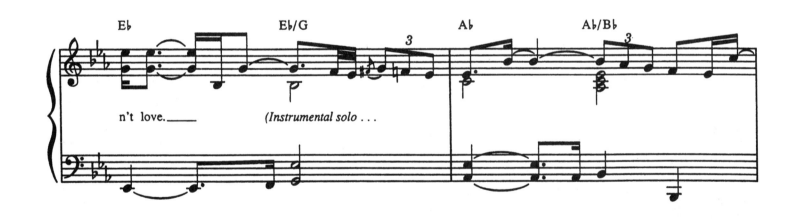

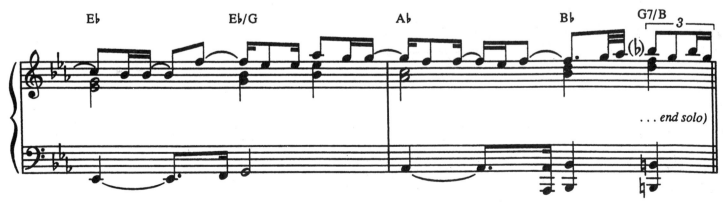

If This Isn't Love - 4 - 4

IN THE HEAT OF THE NIGHT

Lyrics by
ALAN and MARILYN BERGMAN

Music by
QUINCY JONES

IT'S A JUNGLE OUT THERE

(from the television series "Monk")

Words and Music by
RANDY NEWMAN

It's a jun - gle out there.

Dis - or - der and con - fu - sion ev - 'ry - where.

No one seems to care, well, I do. *Hey,* who's in

It's a Jungle Out There - 3 - 1

Theme from the TV Series "L.A. LAW"

L.A. LAW
(Main Title)

Music by MIKE POST

L.A. Law - 3 - 1

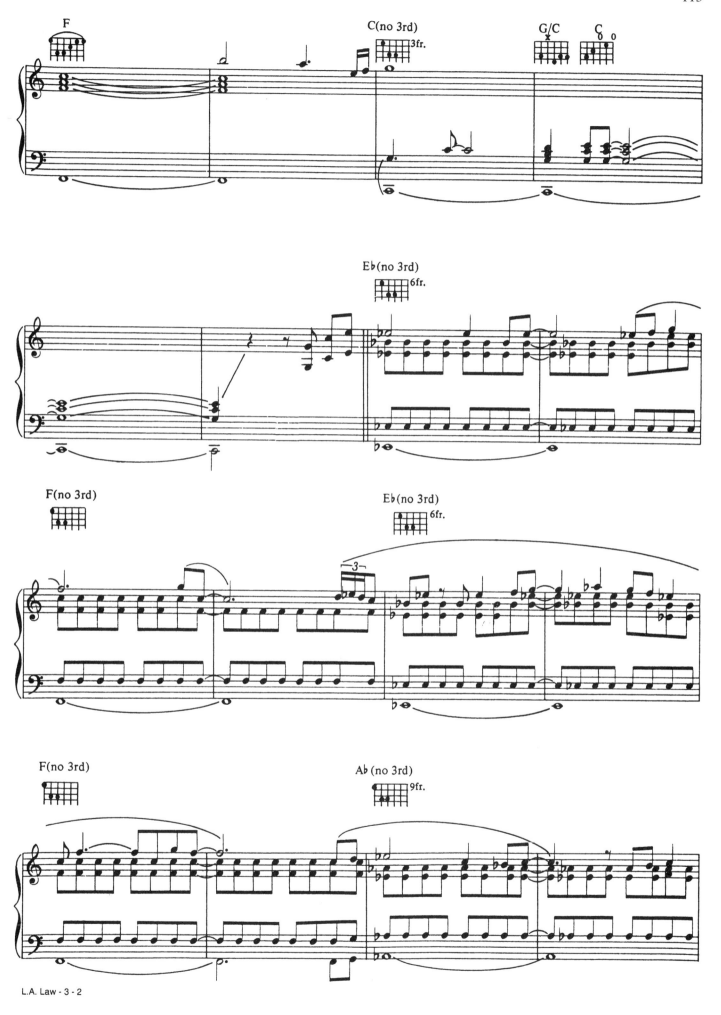

LATE SHOW THEME

By
PAUL SHAFFER

Late Show Theme - 3 - 1

Late Show Theme - 3 - 3

Theme from the PBS Series "MASTERPIECE THEATRE"

THE MASTERPIECE

By
J.J. MOURET and
PAUL PARNES

The Masterpiece - 3 - 1

120

The Masterpiece - 3 - 3

From the WARNER BROS. TV Show "THE DREW CAREY SHOW"

MOON OVER PARMA

(Main Title)

Words and Music by
ROBERT F. McGUIRE

Moon o-ver Par-ma, bring my love to me to-night.
Moon o-ver Par-ma, shine on I two seven-ty-one.

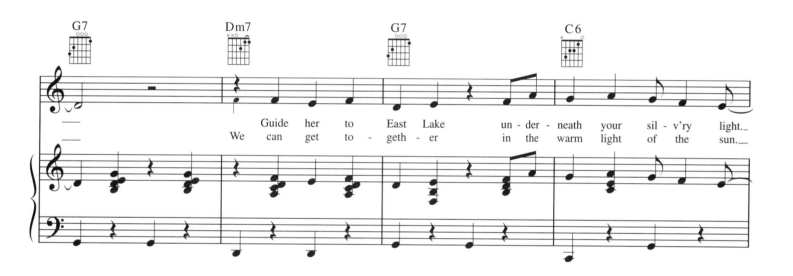

Guide her to East Lake un-der-neath your sil-v'ry light.
We can get to-geth-er in the warm light of the sun.

We met in Ash-ta-bu-la. She was do-in' the
I'm ask-in' you, don't fail. Get her safe-ly through

Moon over Parma - 3 - 1

Moon over Parma - 3 - 3

MICKEY MOUSE MARCH

Words and Music by
JIMMIE DODD

Main Title to the TV Show "THE JEFFERSONS"
MOVIN' ON UP

Words and Music by
JEFF BARRY and
JANET DUBOIS

Movin' on Up - 3 - 1

up   to   the   east_____   side.

We   fin - 'ly   got   a   piece   of   the   pie.__

__   Fish   don't   fry   in   the   kitch - en;

beans   don't   burn   on   the   grill.   Took a - whole__ lot o' try - in'

Movin' on Up - 3 - 2

Theme from the Television Production "MR. LUCKY"

MR. LUCKY

Words by JAY LIVINGSTON and RAY EVANS
Music by HENRY MANCINI

Mr. Lucky - 3 - 1

130

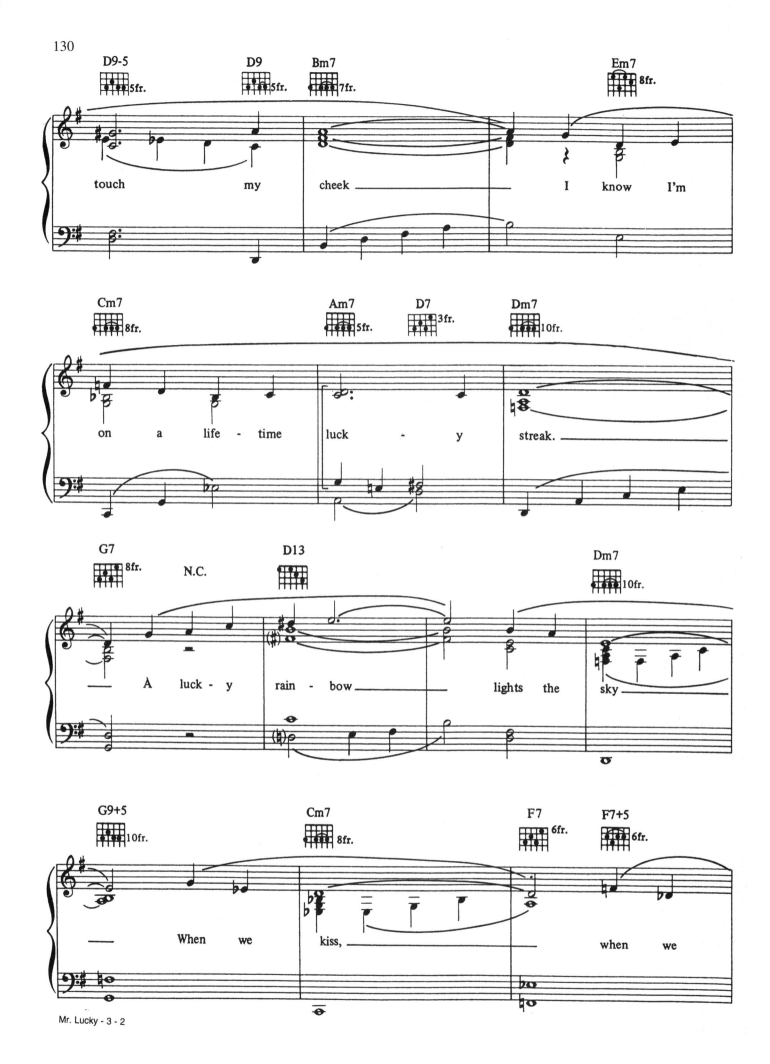

Mr. Lucky - 3 - 2

131

Mr. Lucky - 3 - 3

Theme From the PBS Television Series "MYSTERY"
MYSTERY

Music by
NORMAND ROGER

Mystery - 3 - 1

Mystery - 3 - 2

134

Mystery - 3 - 3

Theme from the TV Series "PETER GUNN"

PETER GUNN

By
HENRY MANCINI

Peter Gunn - 3 - 1

(R.H. ad lib. solo if desired)

loco

Peter Gunn - 3 - 3

Theme From the TV Series "ONE DAY AT A TIME"

ONE DAY AT A TIME

Words and Music by
JEFF BARRY and NANCY BARRY

One Day at a Time - 2 - 1

THE PINK PANTHER

Music by
HENRY MANCINI

The Pink Panther - 2 - 1

The Pink Panther - 2 - 2

SATURDAY NIGHT LIVE
(Opening and Closing Theme)

Opening Theme

Composed by
HOWARD SHORE

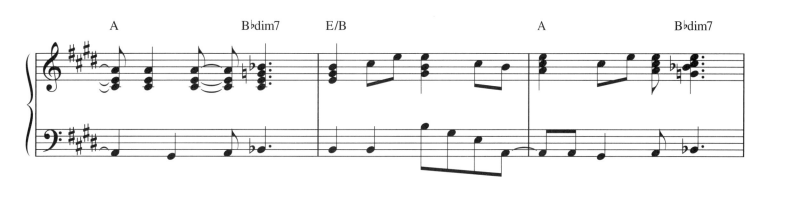

Saturday Night Live - 7 - 2

Closing Theme

Rubato, gospel feel ($\quarternote = 92$)

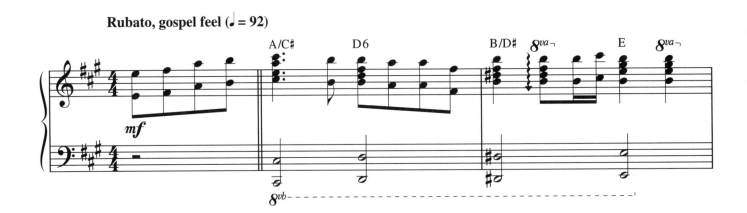

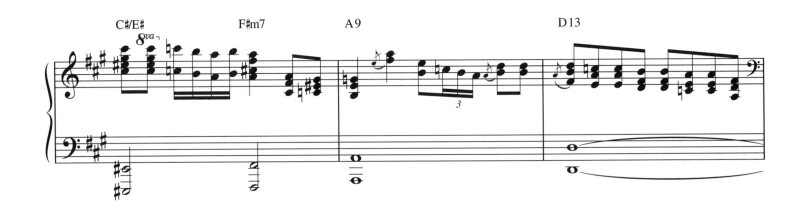

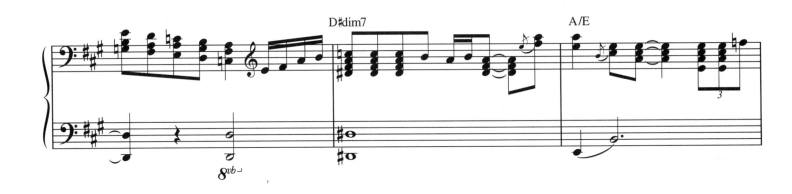

146

Saturday Night Live - 7 - 5

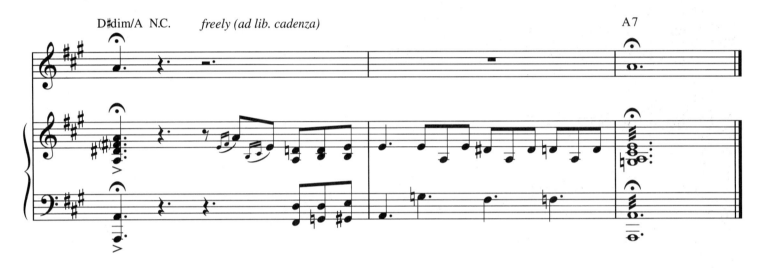

SONG FROM M*A*S*H

(Suicide Is Painless)

Lyric by MIKE ALTMAN

Music by JOHNNY MANDEL

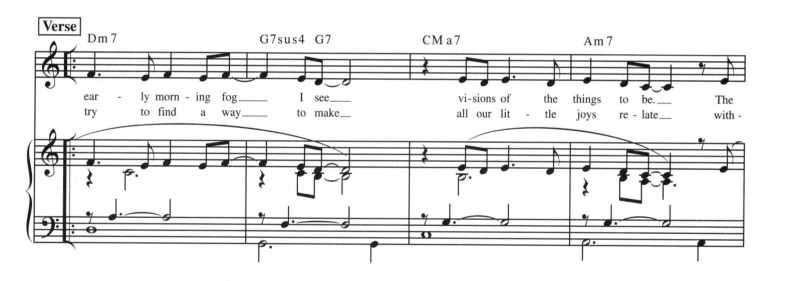

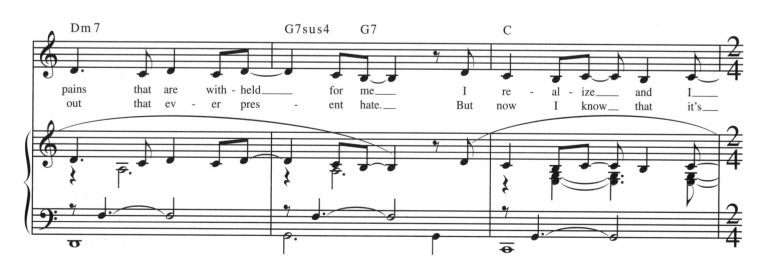

Song from M*A*S*H - 3 - 1

Rubato - Slowly

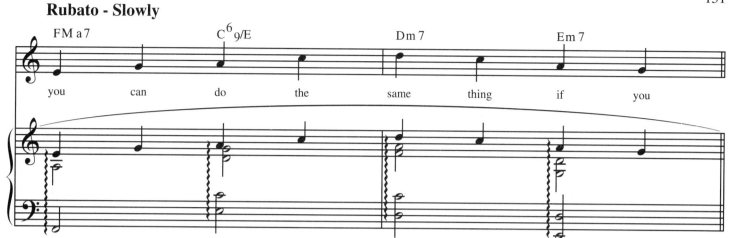

you can do the same thing if you

A Tempo

please.

rall.... *molto*

3. The game of life is hard to play.
 I'm going to lose it anyway.
 The losing card I'll someday lay,
 so this is all I have to say.
  That: (chorus)

4. The only way to win, is cheat
 and lay it down before I'm beat,
 and to another give a seat
 for that's the only painless feat.
  'Cause (chorus)

5. The sword of time will pierce our skins.
 It doesn't hurt when it begins,
 but as it works its way on in,
 the pain grows stronger, watch it grin.
  For: (chorus)

6. A brave man once requested me
 to answer questions that are key.
 Is it to be or not to be?
 And I replied; "Oh, why ask me?"
  'Cause (chorus)

SCOOBY-DOO MAIN TITLE
from the Cartoon Television Series

Words and Music by
WILLIAM HANNA, JOSEPH BARBERA
and HOYT CURTAIN

The Opening Title Theme from the HBO® series,
SEX AND THE CITY

SEX AND THE CITY
(Main Title Theme)

Music Composed by
DOUGLAS J. CUOMO

Bright latin ♩ = 157

Sex and the City - 2 - 1

155

Sex and the City - 2 - 2

From the Peter Jones Production

THEME FROM STARDUST:
THE BETTE DAVIS STORY

Music by EARL ROSE

(pedal simile)

157

Theme From Stardust: The Bette Davis Story - 2 - 2

STARGATE SG-1™

Music by
DAVID ARNOLD

Stargate SG-1™ - 2 - 1

THE SYNCOPATED CLOCK

By
LEROY ANDERSON

The Syncopated Clock - 4 - 1

raved and raved, be-cause no-bod-y could say   why his sil-ly clock be-haved that

hick-o-ry dick-o-ry   way.   But   now   a   fa-mous man   is he,_   He

owns   a   pub-lic   cu-ri-os-i-ty; From far and wide the peo-ple flock To hear THE SYN-CO-

PAT-ED CLOCK.   Tick-a-

162

tock,   tick-a-tock,   There's a zing in the swing of that clock,   Tock-a-

tick,   tock-a-tick,   Don't you think it's a mar-vel-ous trick?   Ting-a-

ling,   ting-a-ling,   There's a zong in the bong of that ring,   Ling-a-

ting,   ling-a-ting,   Don't you think it's a won-der-ful thing?   The

The Syncopated Clock - 4 - 3

ex-perts came to hear and see, But none of them could solve the mys-ter-y, They called Pro-fes-sor Ein-stein too, He said "There's noth-ing I can do." But soon the fick-le hu-man race will find an-oth-er freak to take its place, And one fine day the man will hock the poor old SYN-CO-PAT-ED CLOCK.

The Syncopated Clock - 4 - 4

Main Title From "HOPE & GLORIA"

THANK GOD FOR A FRIEND LIKE YOU

Words by
CHERI STEINKELLNER

Music by
CRAIG SAFAN

Moderate rock ♩ = 126

THE JETSONS (MAIN THEME)

Words and Music by
WILLIAM HANNA, JOSEPH BARBERA
and HOYT CURTIN

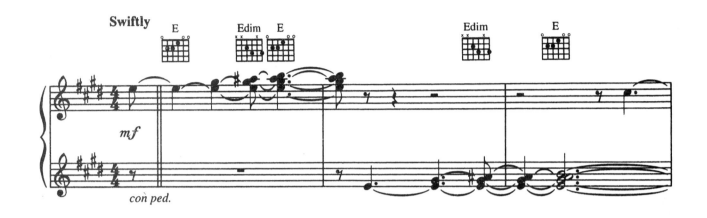

Meet George Jet - son!

The Jetsons (Main Theme) - 3 - 1

168

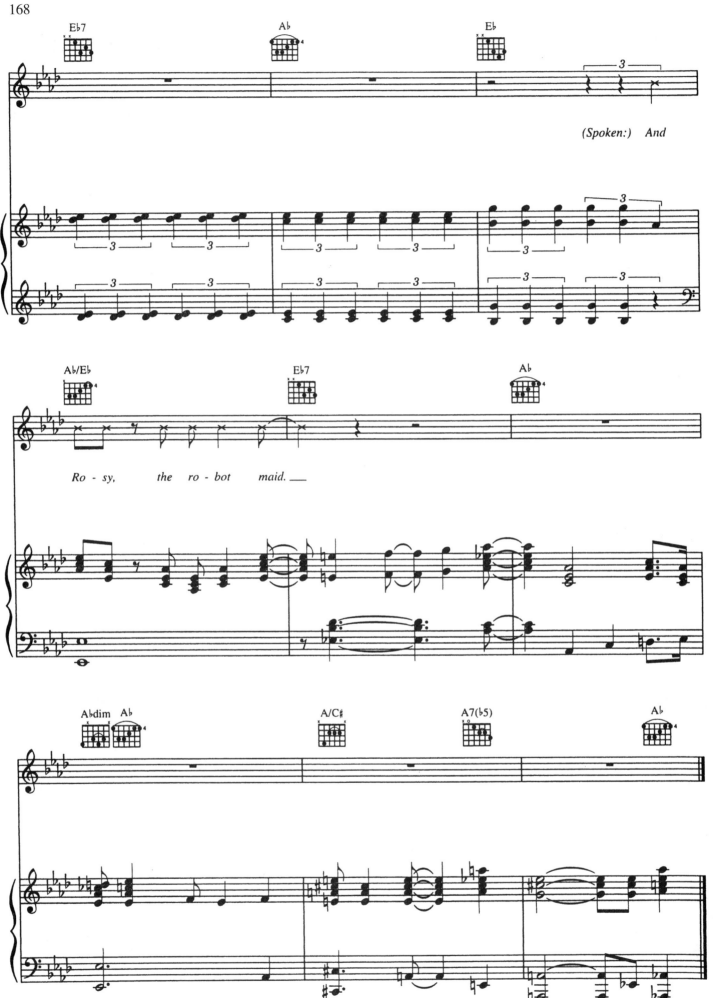

The Jetsons (Main Theme) - 3 - 3

JOSIE AND THE PUSSYCATS (MAIN TITLE)
(From The Cartoon Television Series)

Words and Music by
HOYT CURTIN, DENBY WILLIAMS
and JOSEPH ROLAND

Josie and the Pussycats (Main Title) - 3 - 1

170

THEME FROM F-TROOP

Words by
IRVING TAYLOR

Music by
WILLIAM LAVA

Bright Snappy March

When -

ev - er they hail the Ca - val - ry, they sing of a cer - tain group; but
In - di - ans come to make a raid, no In - di - an gives a whoop; for

no - bod - y men - tions brav - er - y, for there's nev - er been an - y in "F"
In - di - an braves are all a - fraid the noise - 'll a - rouse and a - wake "F"

Theme From F-Troop - 2 - 1

THEME FROM "CHiPs"

From the MGM-TV Series

Music by
JOHN CARL PARKER

Theme From "CHiPs" - 3 - 1

Theme From "CHiPs" - 3 - 2

176

THEME FROM
"HARDCASTLE AND McCORMICK"

(Drive)

Lyrics by
STEVE GEYER

Music by
MIKE POST

Moderately fast rock ♩ = 138

Drive! _____ Push it to the floor 'til the en - gine screams. _____

Drive! _____ Driv-ing like the de - mon that drives your dreams. _____ You're on a

hard road, no-bod-y cares _ if you hit the brakes. _

_ You've got to think fast, keep it in gear. _ One

Theme From "Hardcastle and McCormick" - 3 - 1

178

bet - tin' your life ___ on the state - of - the - art. Lay down the law. ___

Don't you let 'em cross the line. ___

Un - der the hood, ___ got the bad ___ and the good. Ev - ery-bod-y's do - in' time. ___

D.C. al Coda

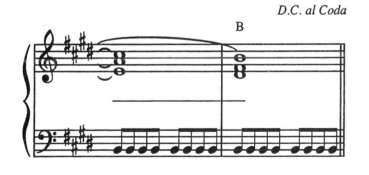

Coda

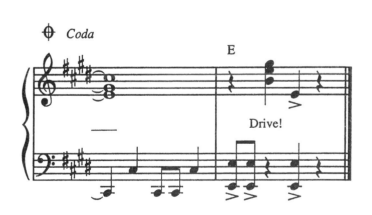

Drive!

Theme From "Hardcastle and McCormick" - 3 - 3

A 20th Century-Fox Series

THEME FROM "PEYTON PLACE"

Lyric by
PAUL FRANCIS WEBSTER

Music by
FRANZ WAXMAN

Theme From "Peyton Place" - 2 - 1

THEME FROM "HUNTER"

Music by
MIKE POST and PETE CARPENTER

Theme From "Hunter" - 3 - 1

184

THEME FROM "THE A-TEAM"

Words and Music by
MIKE POST and PETE CARPENTER

Theme From "The A-Team" - 3 - 1

186

Theme From "The A-Team" - 3 - 2

Theme From "The A-Team" - 3 - 3

From the TV Series "FANTASY ISLAND"

THEME FROM FANTASY ISLAND

Music by
LAURENCE ROSENTHAL

Theme From Fantasy Island - 3 - 1

Theme From Fantasy Island - 3 - 2

190

Theme From Fantasy Island - 3 - 3

(Theme from)
THE ROSIE O'DONNELL SHOW

Words by
RANDY COHEN

Music by
JOHN McDANIEL

The Rosie O'Donnell Show - 3 - 1

192

THEME FROM "GREATEST AMERICAN HERO"

(Believe It Or Not)

Lyrics by
STEVE GEYER

Music by
MIKE POST

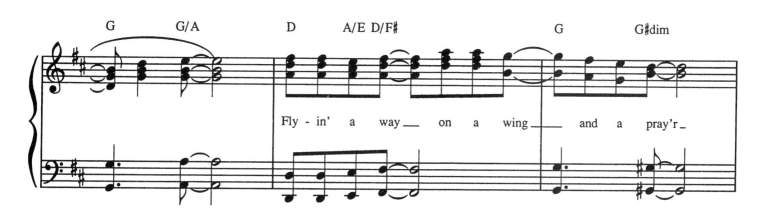

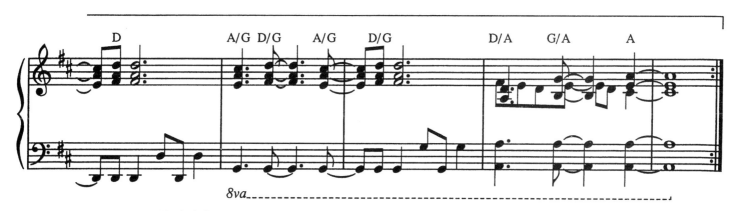

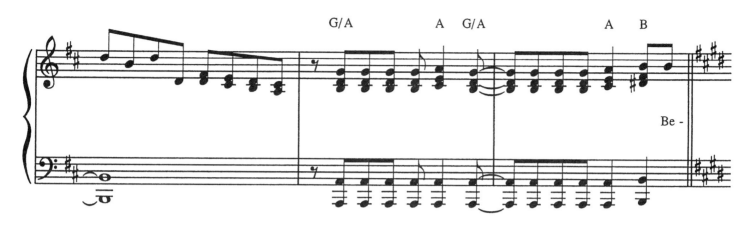

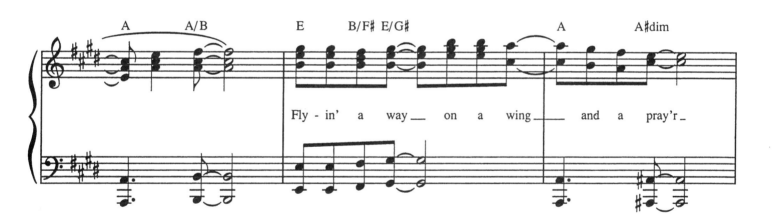

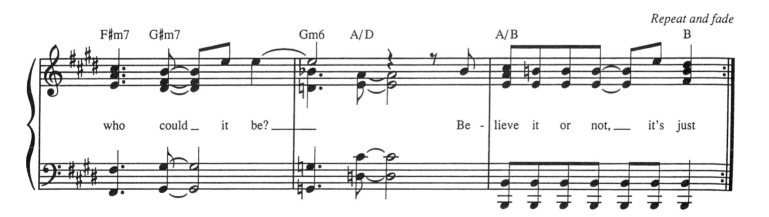

Theme From "Greatest American Hero" - 4 - 4

THEME FROM "THE ROAD RUNNER"

By
BARBARA CAMERON

March tempo

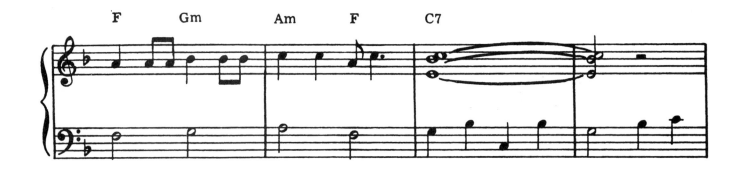

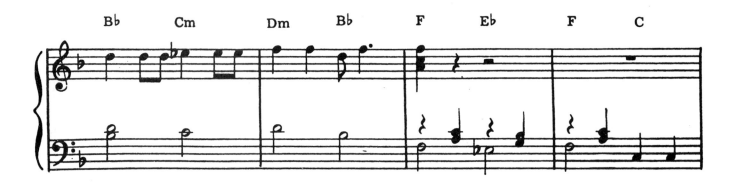

Theme From "The Road Runner" - 2 - 1

Theme From "The Road Runner" - 2 - 2

From the MGM-TV & NBC -TV Prduction "DR. KILDARE"

THEME FROM "DR. KILDARE"

(Three Stars Will Shine Tonight)

Lyric by
HAL WYNN

Music by
JERRALD GOLDSMITH
and PETE RUGOLO

Theme from "Dr. Kildare" - 2 - 1

THEME FROM ZORRO

Words by
NORMAN FOSTER

Music by
GEORGE BRUNS

Theme from Zorro - 3 - 1

THIRTYSOMETHING
(Main Title Theme)

By W.G. "Snuffy" WALDEN
and STEWART LEVIN

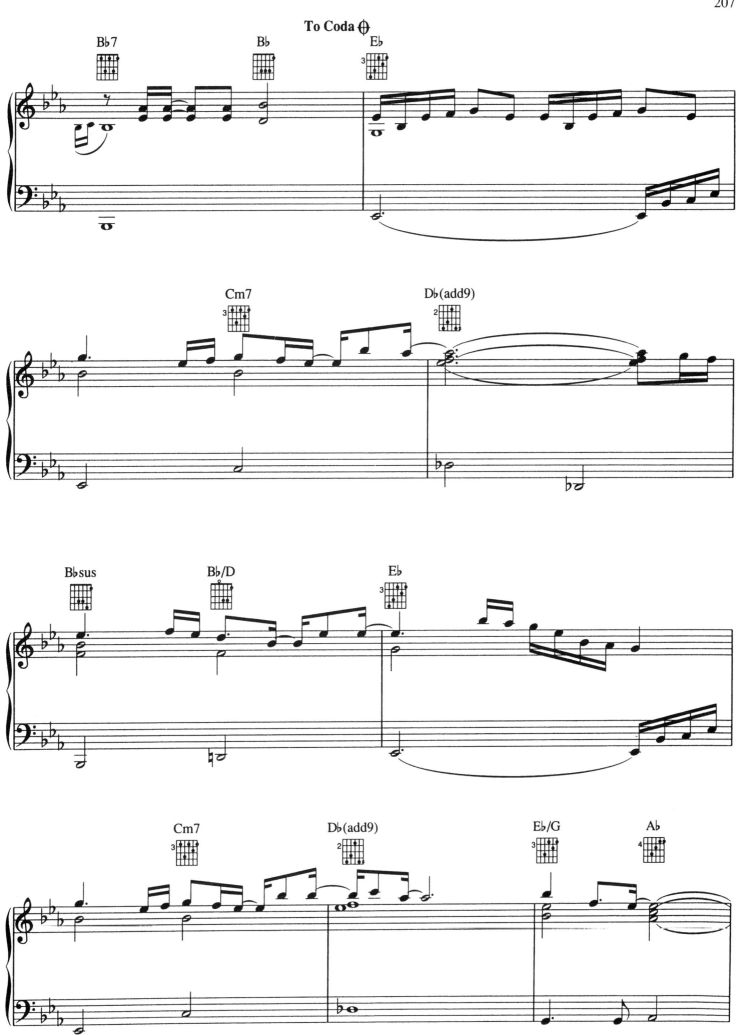

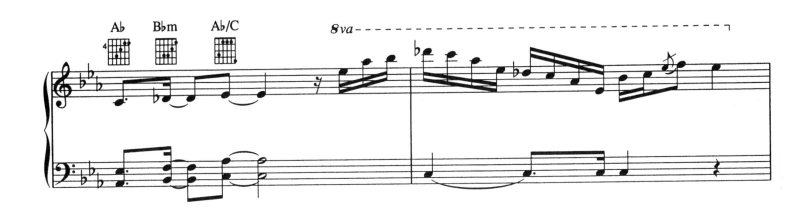

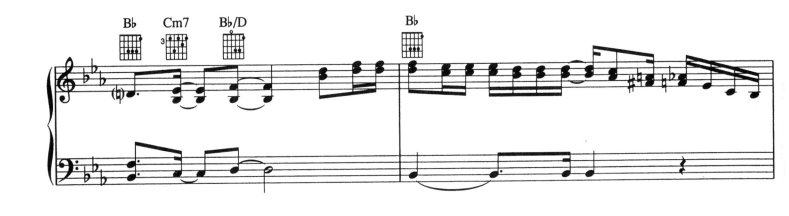

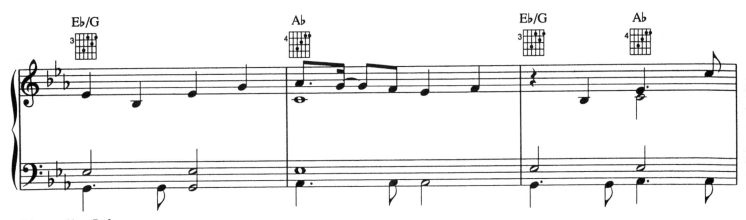

Thirtysomething - 7 - 7

THEME FROM "WISEGUY"

Music by
MIKE POST

Moderate rock ♩ = 126

Theme From "Wiseguy" - 4 - 1

Theme From the TV Show "ALL IN THE FAMILY"

THOSE WERE THE DAYS

Words by
LEE ADAMS

Music by
CHARLES STROUSE

Those Were the Days - 3 - 1

Those Were the Days - 3 - 2

218

Those Were the Days - 3 - 3

Theme from *"THE BUGS BUNNY SHOW"*

THIS IS IT!

Words and Music by
MACK DAVID and JERRY LIVINGSTON

This Is It! - 3 - 1

220

From the "TONY ORLANDO & DAWN SHOW"

TIE A YELLOW RIBBON
'ROUND THE OLE OAK TREE

Words and Music by
IRWIN LEVINE and L. RUSSELL BROWN

1. I'm com - in' home, I've done my time, now I've got to know what is and is - n't mine. If

2. Bus driv - er please look for me, 'cause I could - n't bear to see what I might see. I'm

Tie a Yellow Ribbon 'Round the Ole Oak Tree - 4 - 1

Tie a Yellow Ribbon 'Round the Ole Oak Tree - 4 - 2

224

Tie a Yellow Ribbon 'Round the Ole Oak Tree - 4 - 3

Tie a Yellow Ribbon 'Round the Ole Oak Tree - 4 - 4

TURN IT ALL AROUND

Words and Music by
ROXANNE SEEMAN
and BILLIE HUGHES

Turn It All Around - 5 - 1

As Performed by THE TORIES

TIME FOR YOU
(Main Title from "JESSE")

Words and Music by
STEVE BERTRAND, J.J. FARRIS
and MICHAEL SKLOFF

Tune guitar down 1/2 step:

⑥ = E♭   ③ = G♭
⑤ = A♭   ② = B♭
④ = D♭   ① = E♭

*E is enharmonic chord spelling of F♭.

Time for You - 3 - 1

Time for You - 3 - 3

From the NBC Production "LATE NIGHT WITH DAVID LETTERMAN"

VIEWER MAIL THEME

Music by
HENRY MANCINI

Viewer Mail Theme - 2 - 1

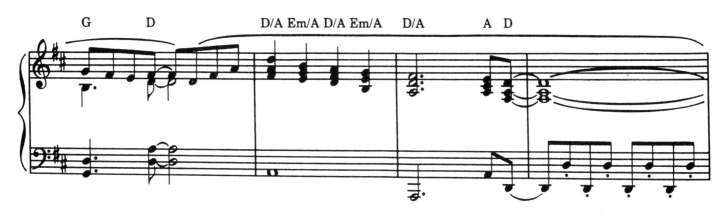

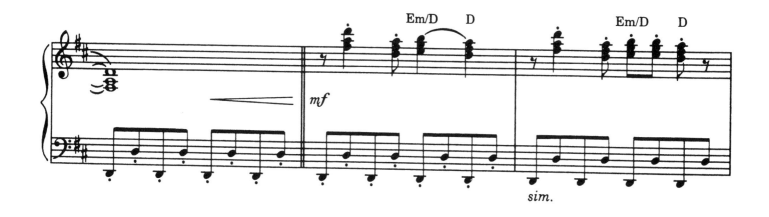

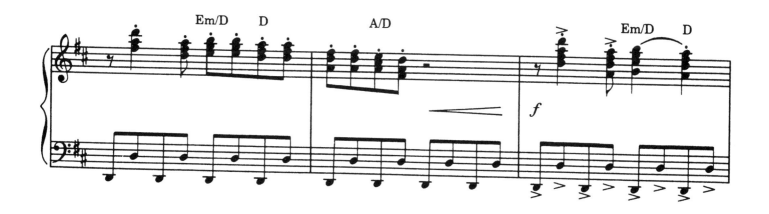

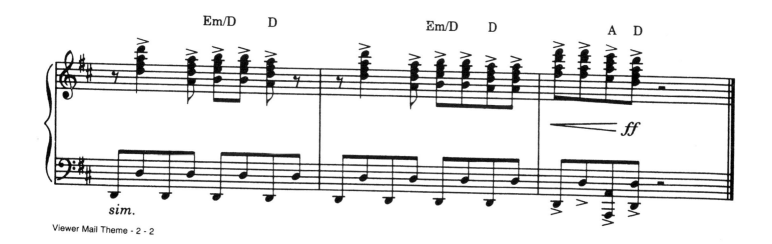

Viewer Mail Theme - 2 - 2

WALLS OF LOVE

Words and Music by
ROXANNE SEEMAN and BILLIE HUGHES

Moderately ♩ = 96

1. Well, it's

Verse:

break - in' me___ to see you here a - gain.___ I'm___
(2.) wis - er now,___ and I know so much___ more,

fall - in'; it's tak - en me___ the world not to give
feel - in'. I'll take you slow,___ but how come when, be -

238

Walls of Love - 4 - 3

WELCOME TO THE EDGE

Words and Music by
ROXANNE SEEMAN, BILLIE HUGHES
and DOMINIC MESSINGER

242

Welcome to the Edge - 4 - 3

244

"Emmy® Award winner for OUTSTANDING ORIGINAL SONG"

WHERE THERE IS HOPE
From the CBS Series "GUIDING LIGHT"

Lyrics by TREY BRUCE,
BRIAN D. SIEWERT
and JOHN BETTIS

Music by
BRIAN D. SIEWERT

*2nd time only.

Where There Is Hope - 5 - 1

Bridge:

cer - tain as___ this mo - ment, as frag - ile as_____ we are,__ there's a

light that drives__ our spir - it burn - ing some - where in the

dark._____

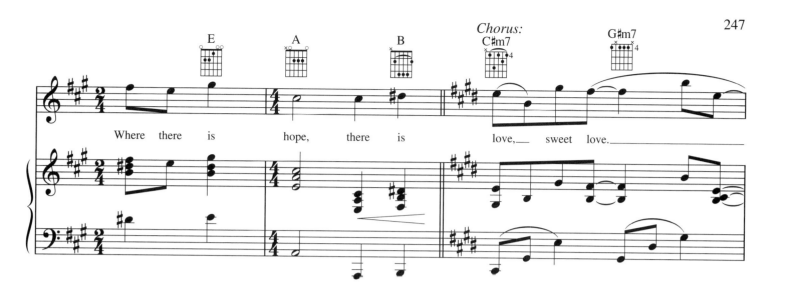

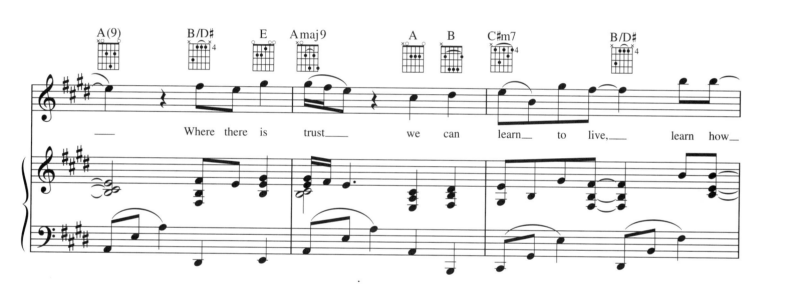

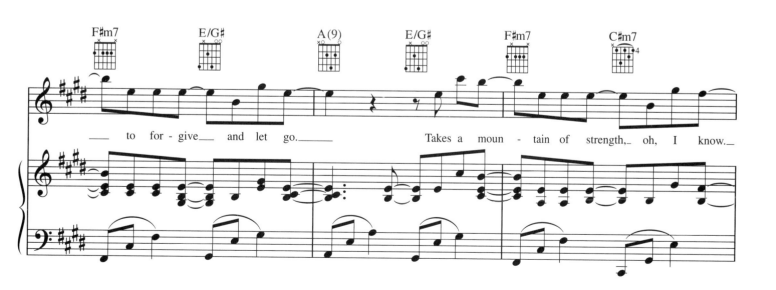

Where There Is Hope - 5 - 4

But love____ finds a way_____ to grow_____ where there is_____

hope._____ On - ly God_____ knows

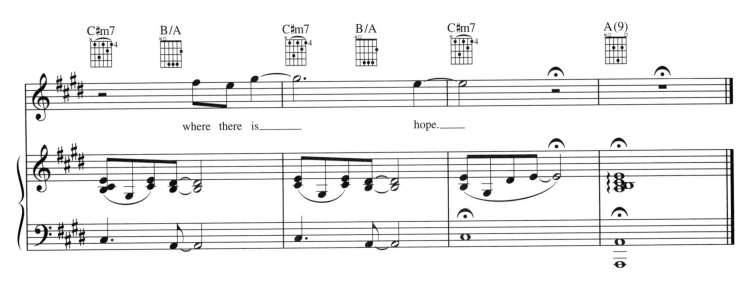

where there is_____ hope._____

From the TV Series "The West Wing"

THE WEST WING (MAIN TITLE)

Composed by
W.G. SNUFFY WALDEN

YOGI BEAR SONG

From the Cartoon Television Series

Words and Music by WILLIAM HANNA
JOSEPH BARBERA and HOYT S. CURTIN

Yo - gi Bear is smart-er than the av - 'rage bear. Yo - gi Bear is al - ways in the rang - er's hair. At a pic - nic ta - ble, you will find him there, stuff - in' down more good-ies than the

Yogi Bear Song - 2 - 1

251

THE YOUNG RIDERS
(Theme)

Composed by
JOHN DEBNEY

Quickly ♩ = 144

(Inst. solo)

The Young Riders - 3 - 1

254

The Young Riders - 3 - 3

WHOSE LINE IS IT ANYWAY?

(Main Theme)

By MARK MATTHEWS,
JAMES GRIFFITH and KATHY MATTHEWS